SCRIPTURE • FOR • LIVING

How Can I Pray?

How Can I Pray?

Ian Petit OSB

DARTON, LONGMAN AND TODD
LONDON

First published in 1991 by
Darton, Longman and Todd Ltd
89 Lillie Road, London SW6 1UD

© 1991 Ian Petit OSB

ISBN 0–232–51947–1

A catalogue record for this book is available
from the British Library

The Scripture quotations are taken from the
New Jerusalem Bible, published and copyright 1985 by
Darton, Longman and Todd Ltd and Doubleday & Co Inc
and used by permission of the publishers

The cover illustration, The Secret Place,
is by Elizabeth Wang.

*'If we turn in prayer to God, and show
him our inmost fears and longings, he will daily
encourage us to return to that secret place
in our hearts where his love is at work.'*

Phototypeset in 10/12 pt Trump by Intype, London
Printed and bound in Great Britain by
Courier International Ltd, East Kilbride, Scotland

Contents

Introduction

━━

THE WRITINGS OF THE BIBLE – the Scriptures – are the Word of God. They are of supreme importance to all Christians and to all who wish to know and understand the meaning of Christianity. The Bible should be in every Christian home. Every aspect of Christian life and worship should reflect in some way what God says to his people. Catholics have not always been very good at reading and studying the Bible. In 1965 during the Second Vatican Council a document on Scripture as the Word of God (*Dei Verbum*) was published. This has had a marked effect in laying the foundations for an official programme of encouragement to Catholics to make the Bible central to their lives.

Much has happened since then. Every public act of worship has its readings from Scripture. Scripture (both Old and New Testaments) has a significant place in all religious education programmes, whether for adults or for children. The lectionary for the readings at daily and Sunday Mass covers a large amount of Scripture during its three-year cycle. Familiar acts of devotion like the Rosary and the Stations of the Cross have become far more scripturally based.

The positive value of this is obvious enough. But it has also meant that many Catholics have been thrown in at the deep end. They are a little like the Ethopian in his carriage on the way home from Jerusalem who was reading some Scripture. Philip the Deacon heard him and asked him if he understood what he was reading. 'How can I', the man said, 'unless I have someone to guide me?' (Acts 8:26–40). Most of us do need help if we are to understand what we are reading. It is not that the language of Scripture is particularly difficult; it is rather that its context is so often unfamiliar.

I warmly welcome this series of *Scripture for Living*. Its particular value is that it helps us to see how Scripture is relevant to our daily lives. There are many other books for scholars. This series is for ordinary Christians who treasure Scripture, know for certain that it is of fundamental importance, but who are not sure how to make sense of what they read or how to relate it to their daily lives and experiences.

The pattern of the series is story, bible passage, commentary, reflection and prayer. There is a natural progression in this. The writings in the Bible (which form a whole library really) are about people trying to recognise God in their lives. So the context is just everyday life – the stuff of story. Story leads on naturally to Scripture because Scripture is itself about life in all its variety. So it speaks of love and hate, success and failure, death and resurrection; almost every imaginable human failing and strength finds place in it, simply because it is about real people. The commentary is an aid to understanding. Then, since the ultimate purpose of Scripture is to lead people closer to God, the text finishes with a prayer which ties together what has gone before and shows how our daily lives can be enriched.

The series is ideal for use in groups as well as by individuals. I wish it every success.

+ DAVID KONSTANT
Bishop of Leeds

Preface

I FEEL SOMEWHAT SHY in being asked to write this book because I do not see myself as a successful prayer. I have struggled for years at prayer and have known much heartache and discouragement, and I have ended up with some very simple thoughts on the subject. I know when I pray that God is present. It makes no difference if I feel he is there. The fact is that he *is* there and he has promised to be there. The other important truth I have discovered is that prayer is not to be judged by what I have got out of it, nor even by what I have put into it; it does not matter if I have had great thoughts or no thoughts, for prayer is not really about thinking; what matters is whether I have tried to love the Lord.

Prayer for me is constantly relating to God. I try not to confine it to special moments, though obviously there are special times when I try deliberately to pray. I seek to make the whole of my life a relating to God. You cannot form a proper relationship with someone to whom you never speak. Prayer is a dialogue, with God speaking first. But how do we hear God speak? Some people actually do hear God's voice in some inexplicable way – I don't. The way he communicates with me is through nature, through Scripture, through the ups and downs of life. What manner of being must he be who made sunlight, colours, hills and rainbows? Whenever I look at something beautiful, I try to imagine that God is saying to me, 'Do you like this or that? I made it for you. Did you see the particular blue in the sky this morning or had you forgotten that it is my world you are living in?' Childish? I do not think so, but I agree it may not be the way everyone would or should want to think.

Of course God has a lot more to say than that he is the inventor of beauty. He speaks to us in our tragedies, in our disasters and moments of fear. He speaks to us in our failures, our guilt, our weaknesses. He speaks when we feel most small and lost.

What is most important is our basic picture or idea of God. If God for us is not a loving person, then we can project our own feelings on to him and imagine, for example, that our sense of guilt or smallness are God condemning us. In such instances we need to remember the words in Scripture, 'Neither shall I condemn you'.

We need to ponder all that God has said to us in the Bible, remembering that Scripture has many faces and that we must balance one passage with another; there are plenty of passages, for example, where God appears angry and even harsh, but there are many others where he appears the opposite. God cannot fit into human language, so we must not become preoccupied with words, for words change from one generation to the next, and in translations exact renderings cannot always be made. We need to remember rather that God's words are 'spirit and life' – they have the power to speak to the deepest yearnings of our hearts.

God has spoken to us and we are called to reflect seriously upon his words. We need to develop the art of listening, of discerning when it is our own voice speaking and when it is the Lord's. So do not bring too many of your own ideas to the word of God, but allow the word to speak to you. Ask guidance of the Holy Spirit and then persevere.

IAN PETIT OSB

The Singer and the Song

A SONG EXISTS only as long as the singer chooses to sing it into being. Let's imagine for a moment that a song could have consciousness; in other words, could be aware of itself.

I expect its first reaction would be one of sheer delight and amazement at its own form of existence. What an extraordinary thing to have one's being stretched out over time. No one moment can contain all of you, so existence means being passed from second to second, with no stopping to enjoy the richer bits nor rushing over what seems more unpleasant. A song cannot be had all at once, it has to come moment by moment. It is the sum of all the moments, and yet each moment is not the whole song.

Songs rise and fall. Sometimes they ascend with a sense of majesty and awe, lifting us up to celestial heights, rising slowly from note to note. Others soar up rapidly like swallows in a summer sky and then come plummetting down leaving us all but breathless.

A song, gifted with consciousness, would be fascinated with itself. How it would delight in winging down the scales, rising to dizzy heights and crashing into growling depths. What moods! What wonder! What beauty!

Hopefully, one day, the song would begin to ask where it comes from. Clearly it does not cause itself to exist. It receives existence moment by moment, but where does the gift of being come from? No sooner has it received one moment than there is another offered, and so it goes on.

The time when the song begins to ask this fundamental question, would, I think, be a time of both vulnerability and joy. Vulnerability, because it would suddenly know its own fragility; it does not depend on itself for life. What if the one who makes it exist should cease to bring it into being? I am sure there would be a momentary wobble as the song discovers the truth of its dependence on another.

Yet a deeper, more joyful and more comforting thought would no doubt dawn – 'I do exist, therefore someone must want me to be'. What an extraordinary comfort for the song to know that it is wanted. Existence is not of its own making, another has chosen it and goes on choosing it. I am sure the song would then want to know something about the singer. Is he or she good, strong, wise, powerful, loving? Now the song would begin to look beyond itself towards the singer. What manner of being must he or she be?

But could a song learn anything about the singer? A song only has song-experience and could not begin even to wonder what the singer would be like.

The only way that this could happen would be for the singer to tell the song about himself or herself.

In the beginning God created heaven and earth. Now the earth was a formless void, there was darkness over the deep, with a divine wind sweeping over the waters . . .

God said, 'Let us make man in our own image, in the likeness of ourselves, and let them be masters of the fish of the sea, the birds of heaven, the cattle, all the wild animals and all the creatures that creep along the ground.'

> *God created man in the image of himself,*
> *in the image of God he created him,*
> *male and female he created them.*

God blessed them, saying to them, 'Be fruitful, multiply, fill the earth and subdue it. Be masters of the fish of the sea, the birds of heaven and all the living creatures that move on earth.' God also said, 'Look, to you I give all the seed-bearing plants everywhere on the surface of the earth, and all the trees with seed-bearing fruit; this will be your food. And to all the wild animals, all the birds of heaven and all the living creatures that creep along the ground, I give all the foliage of the plants as their food.' And so it was. God saw all he had made, and indeed it was very good. Evening came and morning came: the sixth day.

(Genesis 1: 1–2, 26–31)

God has made everything. He spoke and things suddenly came into being. The fact that they have remained in being must mean that he continues to speak, or sing, them. We could therefore say that he is continually singing creation into being. I find this a wonderful way to think of creation – as God's song.

We, of course, are among the things that God sings into being. Each one of us is different, unique. God has specially chosen us, and it is important for us to remember that God never makes a mistake. We are his invention, and he goes on inventing us at every moment.

It is sad that so many of us often have very bad pictures of ourselves. Certainly, we have made mistakes, done wrong things, but to judge ourselves by our errors and misdeeds is to value ourselves by what we do and not by what we are. We are the special creation of God and as such we are of immense value.

I find it helpful sometimes to seek out a quiet place to sit and just ponder from where my life is coming. We certainly do not cause our own existence – if we did that, then we could guarantee that we would see the next century in. We need to try and be aware of receiving existence as a gift and let ourselves be amazed that God has chosen to create us. We know how much we like to be thanked when we give something to someone, so it perhaps isn't too difficult to imagine the joy God must feel when we thank him for calling us into being.

Returning to the idea of the song, imagine how foolish it would be if the song turned round to the singer and said, 'I do not need you'. What an insult that would be! That is what sin is. Sin is us saying to the God who creates us, 'I do not need you'. *All* sin involves us trying to be independent of God.

I realise that when we pray it is not easy for us to focus on these deeper truths. We live in a busy world and there are so many demands made upon us. There is always this need and that, there is the constant pressure of time. We are continually being pushed to hurry and fit everything in. That is why it is so necessary to try and be still and stand back from life so that we may look and see things in perspective.

Being still is difficult. Our minds are so active. We may be used to 'thinking' about God, but prayer is really more about 'loving' God and being open to him. That is why it is good to try and become aware of the actual moment we are living. To be conscious of what we feel, be aware of what we sense at this very moment. If we concentrate on experiencing all these sensations as God speaking to us, we will find that our attention can become focused. Hopefully, just as the song did, we will begin to ask, 'Who is calling us into being?' 'What is he like?' We will discover that we want to know our creator, and to build a relationship with him.

FOR REFLECTION

1. Do you want to discover and know God, the one who sings you into being?
2. Do you want to build a relationship with him?
3. Do you have a set time for prayer, or are you hoping to fit it in 'sometime', or do you leave it until you have some urgent need?
4. How much of your prayer time is spent in thanksgiving?
5. You may, like me, find it helpful to be quiet for a few minutes and concentrate on being open to God in the present moment – open, for example, to your own body, to what you see and hear around you.

PRAYER

Lord, you are the inventor of rainbows, fountains, butterflies and stars. You also chose to invent me. I thank you for my being. I am sorry that I have so misunderstood you – I have been so very blind.

I know you are listening to me right now and through your Son's cross you have forgiven me and your Holy Spirit brings me that forgiveness because I am asking for it. Help me to see you in every event of this day. You are my creator, and I say 'yes' to being your creature.

I make this prayer in the name of Jesus Christ your Son. Amen.

Prayer as Listening

⬅➡

MARTIN FELT very low as he tried with no success to keep his mind on God.

He had come on this prayer weekend at the suggestion of Gerard, his friend, who unfortunately had had to cry off at the very last minute. Martin wanted to cancel as well but Gerard had said that he really had no good excuse. So, very reluctantly, Martin had arrived. He knew, as soon as he got there, that he had made a mistake. He did not know a soul, he was by far the youngest, and he was the only man present. Also from what people were saying during the first meal, he felt he was among experts in the art of prayer. People were talking about St Teresa of Avila, St John of the Cross and everyone was asking about a book just out written by a French mystic.

Martin seriously wanted to know more about prayer. Gerard had been on a similar weekend last year and had come home full of it. This had aroused Martin's interest. Martin was 23 and he had felt that there must be much more to prayer than long lists of requests. He had learnt to say the rosary at school, but he never got very much from it. There was always the problem of trying to think of one of the mysteries while you were saying something else. So, because of Gerard's enthusiasm, Martin decided he had better take some steps to learn more about prayer.

The priest, Father Peter, was bald and rather fat, a jolly sort who seemed to have lots to say and many stories to tell. During the first talk on the Friday evening he said, and it seemed as though he said it almost by chance, that prayer involved listening to God not just talking to him. Though Martin would not have said that that was a totally new idea to him, in some way it struck him. In fact it struck him so forcibly that he decided, there and then, that he would spend some time next day listening to God.

So here he was in the chapel and he was feeling very low because he did not, or could not, hear God. He had been there for twenty minutes; he had promised to spend half an hour, and nothing had happened. He had started off by asking God to speak to him and had asked pardon for never really trying to hear him before. If the truth were known, he never had expected God to speak to him. Surely God only spoke to exceptionally holy people. Anyway, the priest had said that a large part of prayer was listening to God, so he was giving it a try.

He had been in the chapel about ten minutes when he had heard the door open at the back. For a fleeting moment he wondered if that was God coming in to talk with him, then he dismissed the idea remembering that God was already in the chapel and besides God did not come in through doors.

How incredibly difficult it was to listen and not get distracted. How do you listen to nothing? Was God going to speak in a solemn voice? It was all very well to say that we need to listen, but just how do you do that? He had heard a bus going down the street outside, and half wished that he was on it, back in his normal world. Every now and then the radiators gave a creak, or he could hear someone calling in the distance. A dog barked. An aeroplane flew overhead. In fact he heard nearly everything but God.

Because he could not hear God, he found his thoughts wandering here, there and everywhere. He tried picturing God, but soon gave that up because God is spirit, he has no body, no shape. It was rather difficult picturing someone with no shape. He then tried picturing Jesus. This wasn't successful either because the statue of the Sacred Heart, not far from where he was kneeling, was very different to the Jesus on the cross high above the altar. It was all extremely confusing.

Finally he sat down and hoped that it was still prayer even if he had ceased to kneel. Kneeling was all very well but when you have not done a lot of it, it can be painful.

For these last few minutes, which seemed to go even slower than all the others, he decided to try and think of nothing, hoping that if he succeeded God might pop into his mind. Needless to say this was a total failure. Martin, by now, was feeling frustrated, even a little angry and annoyed. After all he had come on this retreat against his will, he had tried to listen to God. Had God not noticed? Was he really there? If so, why did he say nothing? While he was thinking these thoughts he found that he was looking at the lectern standing in the sanctuary. On it stood the book with all the readings for the Masses throughout the year. It suddenly dawned on Martin that God had spoken and he was asking him: 'Why have you never listened to what I have already said?'

God had communicated with Martin and had been doing it for some time, but Martin had not recognised him because he had never really been listening in the right way.

◆━━━◆

Now, the boy Samuel was serving Yahweh in the presence of Eli; in those days it was rare for Yahweh to speak; visions were uncommon. One day, it happened that Eli was lying down in his room. His eyes were beginning to grow dim, he could no longer see. The lamp of God had not yet gone out, and Samuel was lying in Yahweh's sanctuary, where the ark of God was, when Yahweh called, 'Samuel! Samuel!' He answered, 'Here I am,' and, running to Eli, he said, 'Here I am, as you called me.' Eli said, 'I did not call. Go back and lie down.' So he went and lay down. And again Yahweh called, 'Samuel! Samuel!' He got up and went to Eli and said, 'Here I am, as you called me.' He replied, 'I did not call, my son; go back and lie down.' As yet, Samuel had no knowledge of Yahweh and the word of Yahweh had not yet been revealed to him. Again Yahweh called, the third time. He got up and went to Eli and said, 'Here I am, as you called me.' Eli then understood that Yahweh was calling the child, and he said to Samuel, 'Go and lie down, and if someone calls say, "Speak, Yahweh; for your servant is listening."'

(1 Samuel 3:1–9)

◆━━━━▶

Clearly, Samuel did not recognise God when he spoke to him. Three times he thought it was the High Priest Eli speaking to him. So it is with us, we often do not recognise God when he speaks to us.

Martin had the same problem. The priest had reminded him that prayer involved listening as well as speaking. But Martin needed to be taught how to listen. He expected God to speak in audible words; whereas all the time Martin needed to be reminded that God had already spoken many words and he, Martin, had not paid very much attention to them.

How can you have a relationship with someone you do not know? I live near a railway station and frequently I see one of the porters of the station walking

in the street where I live. I do not know his name, I
know he is a porter but I do not know what he thinks,
what he likes, what makes him happy. To find this
out I would need to talk to him and let him talk to
me. Before I can have a relationship with him, I would
need to know him.

It is the same with God. Too often we try to talk to
the God we do not know. We may imagine we know
some things about this God, but often what we know
bears little resemblance to the real God. We get ideas
about God, ideas which are often of our own making.
We need to remember that no thought that any of us
have *is* God. God cannot be caught or captured by a
thought; no thought of ours has got him wrapped up.

We need to allow God to tell us about himself, and
even though our minds will not be big enough to grasp
the full picture, at least we will not be feeding on some
fantasy but on the truth. We need to fill our minds
with all that God has told us. We need to ponder and
listen to what he has said. In Scripture we learn all
that God has done for us human beings, and the
Church brings out the appropriate readings for the lit-
urgical seasons, helping us to hear what God is saying
to us at the relevant times.

But Scripture is not the only way that God speaks
to us. We need to learn how to read the signs of the
times. What is God saying through the state of the
world at the present moment? We need to listen to the
moods within ourselves. We need to be able to recognise fears, sudden moments of anxiety – what is God
saying to us through these things?

Martin was not able to see why he was fearful of
going on that weekend retreat. He was unaware of the
spiritual battle raging within him. Being ignorant of
God's word, of what God had already said, Martin was
no threat to Satan. Martin was not an evil person, he
was nice, pleasant and respectable; but he did not

know the true God; rather, he knew certain things about God, and as such he was no problem to Satan. But if he should learn the truth, then he might tell others. So Satan played upon Martin, and he sensed a great fear and reluctance about the retreat.

Once a person becomes open to the fact that God has actually said quite a lot, and that he still speaks, then that person needs to learn to discern between his or her own promptings and those of God. Imaginative people can easily be led astray. We have to face the fact that we can still be ambitious, even in the realm of the spirit and spiritual pride is very deadly. In John 10:4, Jesus said that his sheep would follow him 'because they know his voice.' In 1 John 4 we are warned to test the spirits. We may get beautiful and apparently holy ideas, but we need to look and see if we are just building ourselves up, imagining we are God's gift to the world, or are we allowing Jesus to be built up? 'Any spirit which acknowledges Jesus Christ, come in human nature, is from God' (1 John 4:2).

Listening is not easy. Samuel was told to say: 'Speak, Yahweh; for your servant is listening.' We tend to say: 'Listen, Lord, your servant is speaking.' We live in a world full of noise and bustle, and when we settle down to pray, our minds continue to whirl around. Obviously we cannot just stop and empty our minds. The mind cannot not think. You might as well command the eye not to see. But it is good to try and still the mind by giving it something to do. Try and fix your mind on the now, the present moment. Be conscious of what you hear, what you feel now. This helps to quieten us down and we become aware of how unaware we really are. The present moment is the only moment that touches us. We can live our lives fretting about the future, worrying about the past and never being truly alive in the present. Being conscious of our breathing, our bodies, can lead us on to consciousness of the gift of life. Who gives us life? In this sort of stillness, we can begin to hear God calling our name.

FOR REFLECTION

1. When you pray, how do you do it? Do you do all the speaking or do you listen?
2. List the different ways in which you hear God.
3. Do you have a set way of praying or do you just hope you will get 'lift-off'?
4. Has your way of praying changed over the years? Can you see why it has changed?

PRAYER

Lord speak your word over my deafness and blindness. Teach me how to listen and hear you in everything that you have made. Lord, stop the chatter of my mind, where I live my desires. Teach me to long for your kingdom, where your will is what is important. Give me ears to hear your still quiet voice. Amen.

Praying through Creation

❂

I MUST HAVE BEEN about 12 years old when a school friend of mine, whose father was posted in Gibraltar, told me about his summer holidays on the Rock. He must have had a way with words for I know I was enraptured as he described the boat journey, the arrival in blazing sunshine, the narrow streets, the monkeys on the Rock, the oranges and grapes, the swimming and the hot summer days. Here was something completely different to my English experience and I fell in love with travel, the tropics and sunshine all in one fell swoop.

The chances of my travelling abroad were very remote, for foreign travel had not become accessible to ordinary people, so I made do with what I had. I became interested in seasons, and I would watch for the shadow of the sun to decrease, showing me that summer was approaching. I became aware of what grew around me, and wondered what it would be like to live in a place where oranges and grapes grew out-of-doors. I do not know if my memory deceives me or if the summers of long ago were really that fine, but I recall hot summer days with swallows wheeling in blue skies, jugs of cold lemonade, Wall's ice creams bought from a man on a bicycle, long summer evenings. Quite unknown to my friend a whole new world had opened up for me. I met something, or was it

someone, in this new world. I could stand for hours
looking at hills, cornfields neatly stacked with stooks,
waterfalls, flowers. I had become a country man, a
man of nature, though I lived in the suburbs of London.

I wonder, now, if I was meeting God then but simply
never recognised him. The God I met in church seemed
to me rather dull, he seemed full of rules and regu-
lations, and was rather against everything that
appealed to me. So I had a fear of him. What I met
in the fields and hills filled me with awe, reverence,
excitement and wonder. I felt an urge to kick off my
shoes and go and dance in the long grass, but I was a
town boy, so I never dared do such a strange thing.
Now I can say that that would have been a form of
worship.

It has taken most of my life to bring these two
ways of meeting God together. Alas, my early church
experience had so coloured my ideas of God that when
I did meet him in the fields I did not recognise him.
What a joy it was when, later in life, I read in the
psalms such marvelous praise of God for the wonders
he has created. How poetic the book of Job is as he
describes the mysteries of creation. How important it
is that we listen to the God who communicates with
us through such things as colour, shape and size.

◆———▶

Bless Yahweh, my soul,
Yahweh, my God, how great you are!
Clothed in majesty and splendour,
wearing the light as a robe!

You stretch out the heavens like a tent,
build your palace on the waters above,
making the clouds your chariot,
gliding on the wings of the wind,

appointing the winds your messengers,
flames of fire your servants.

You fixed the earth on its foundations,
for ever and ever it shall not be shaken;
you covered it with the deep like a garment,
the waters overtopping the mountains.

At your reproof the waters fled,
at the voice of your thunder they sped away,
flowing over mountains, down valleys,
to the place you had fixed for them;
you made a limit they were not to cross,
they were not to return and cover the earth.

(Psalm 104:1–9)

I have often seen some work of art and have felt a
desire to meet the person who could create such
beauty. In some way that beauty resided in the artist
and I wanted to know him or her. I have sometimes
had my wish and been able to meet the person in
question, and I have to confess that occasionally I have
been disappointed. But somewhere, deep down inside
them, that beauty must have resided.

So, what of God who surrounds us with his works
of art? What manner of being must he be who can
create stars and scatter them in such vast spaces? The
psalms describe him as marshalling them and calling
each one by its name. Standing at night and staring
into the clear sky, fills one with awe and wonder.

What manner of being must he be who created
colour and put it everywhere? How dull life would be
if everything appeared as a black and white photo. I
find it helpful to look at things and try and imagine
them as shades of black and white, and then suddenly
I become aware of their colour. I am continually

surprised and delighted by the world God has created,
surprised by the shapes, colour, beauty, growth, rich-
ness and variety. I find it amazing to think that no
two sunsets are ever the same, to think of the seeds
that are scattered – how prodigious is God's bounty.

For me, God is forever nudging us with his creation.
I know every time I go in an aeroplane, it is as good
as a retreat. I admit there is the thought that this might
be my last act – that is sobering and not to be rejected;
but once I am airborne I become like a child with a
new toy. What a wonder it is to suddenly have your
horizons extended. How fascinating it is to look at
things from above. How tiny we humans are. Also
what excitement there is to view the clouds from
above – they have such marvellous shapes and are so
white!

My meeting with God as the creator of the universe
has done much for me. Early impressions of God are
significant for if they are not palatable, then everything
from then on has a bias. Because the God I heard about
in church seemed so unattractive, then everything that
was connected with him became unappealing to me.
My meeting with God in nature had the advantage
that I did not recognise that this was God whom I was
meeting. Having fallen in love with him unconsciously, it was quite startling to learn later on that I
had fallen in love with God!

Although I didn't realise it at the time, I had actually
been praying as a child when I met God in nature. I
had been unconsciously thanking him and worship-
ping him for all his wonders. Now, as an adult, I know
that it is God I see in the beauty around me and I am
able to respond more fully.

Prayer becomes a response to the God who speaks
first to me, and one of the ways he speaks is through
the natural world.

FOR REFLECTION

1. How conscious are you of the beauty around you?
2. Do you just admire beauty in nature or does it lead you on to thinking about God?
3. Do you thank God for his world?

PRAYER

I bless you Father for all that you have invented. I thank you that you included me in your plan. Help me to be a good steward here on earth. Amen.

Praying through Other People

SHE GOT ON THE BUS about two stops after I did. All this must have happened at least 40 years ago, so many of the details have been lost, but the impact of the encounter is still as clear to me as if it happened yesterday.

She must have been well into her forties – may be as much as fifty – but to my young eyes she was old. She was dumpy, her hair was dyed blond and she was highly made-up. What stands out most clearly in my memory is her hat. I cannot remember so much the shape, it was black but it was simply covered with bright red cherries. They hung all over it and at the slightest movement they bounced up and down. I can remember thinking: 'My good lady, why go out dressed up like that?' – and I dismissed her as a foolish old woman.

The seats on the buses in those days ran the length of the bus, looking in, thus giving plenty of room for standing passengers during the rush hour. She sat down, not quite opposite me, a little to my right, and as the bus lurched off the cherries started to dance and bounce.

On my right sat another woman with a small child on her lap and it did not take him long to notice these shining cherries and he stretched out his chubby hands towards them, opening and closing his little fists. Soon the woman with the cherry hat noticed the little boy stretching out affectionately towards her, and so she nodded her head, and the cherries began a wild dance. Squeals of delight came from the child. The more he squealed, the more she nodded, and soon all the people around were drawn into this happy encounter.

This continued for several stops, then the woman beside me, doing her best to control her enraptured son, said to the woman with the hat: 'Have you any children of your own?' I can still see her smiling under that hat of hers as she said: 'Oh, yes, I had one but I lost him.'

I do not know the story. I do not know how it happened, she never told us, she just sat there under her funny hat, smiling and nodding at the little boy who was all but convulsed with laughter and joy. All I know is that I suddenly saw into that good woman's life, I saw behind the funny exterior, I saw into the sanctuary of her being, and I felt very ashamed at my rash judgement.

I wanted to go and kneel in front of her and tell her of my misjudgement – but you just do not do that sort of thing.

I know I got off that bus a wiser young man than I had got on it. She never spoke one single word to me, yet she taught me a lesson that I have never forgotten. 'Do not judge. You do not know what lies behind the pair of eyes you look into. Everyone has their story.'

Do not judge, and you will not be judged; because the judgements you give are the judgements you will get, and the standard you use will be the standard used for you. Why do you observe the splinter in your brother's eye and never notice the great log in your own? And how dare you say to your brother, 'Let me take that splinter out of your eye,' when, look, there

is a great log in your own? Hypocrite! Take the log
out of your own eye first, and then you will see clearly
enough to take the splinter out of your brother's eye.

(Matthew 7:1–5)

We must not confine God to 'holy times' or 'holy
places'. Jesus lived his life both in the market place
and in the hills where he went to pray. God is always
present to us, communicating with us; it is we who
have consciously to make ourselves aware of his presence. Stupidly we can tend to imagine God is only
present when we think of him.

God manifests himself in many ways and one way
is through the people he has made. We need to learn
the art of penetrating beyond the external to find the
singer of each particular song.

We need to remember that other people are other
people – they are not extensions of ourselves, so we
cannot and must not manipulate them. They are other;
and it is not wrong to be other. They will see things
differently from us, and that is of value because we
cannot see all sides to things.

God has made each one of us and each is different,
unique. Life, with all its ups and downs, forms and
shapes us, can even wound us. So when we meet
people we meet someone chosen by God, who never
makes mistakes, but we are also meeting someone
who has a story to tell, and that story will have left
its imprints, both good and bad.

I was different from the woman with the funny hat.
Surely the hat was not funny to her; maybe the fault
was in me. My mistake was to fail to let her be different, and to judge her for being different.

Again, I come back to basic questions – 'Who is this
God to whom we pray? What is he like?' We can make
God into our own image and likeness. We can forget

he made the world and imagine he is only in churchy places. We can domesticate him, shut him up in a box, put him out of reach, not expect to see him in the market place. Nowadays we see posters of beautiful land or seascapes with some scriptural quotation on them, and while that is fine, again, we must not confine God only to the beautiful. When Jesus came on earth, he did not shun sharing our weakness. He so identified himself with our sorrows that Isaiah prophesied:

> As many people were aghast at him
> – he was so inhumanly disfigured
> that he no longer looked like a man –
> so many nations will be astonished
> and kings will stay tight-lipped before him
> seeing what had never been told them,
> learning what they had not heard before.
>   (Isaiah 52:14,15)

Is the God we pray to only the One we meet in Scripture, or is he also the One we meet in others hidden in a thousand different guises? Sometimes so 'disfigured' that we do not recognise him.

When the Lord tells us not to judge, he does not mean that we should never use our critical faculties. We need to listen to the whole of what the Lord has said to us. He certainly tells us not to judge, but he also tells us to be 'cunning as snakes, and yet innocent as doves' (Matthew 10:16). If someone does wrong, I am not called to overlook the wrong, to pretend it is not there. I have to be honest, I may even have to correct the wrong. What the Lord asks of us is not to judge the person, who does wrong, but to try and understand. We are quite ready to find excuses when we do wrong, but are we as ready to excuse others?

So God comes to us in other people and therefore other people can help us in our prayer. They give us glimpses into the God we cannot see. The woman on the bus had some tragic experience, she had lost her child, I do not know the details. Such an experience would have left a mark. Who is to know whether the red hat was some gallant attempt on her part to face life again and appear healed? How thoughtless it was of me to have judged her. She never spoke a word to me, but through her God taught me not to judge. 'You do not know the story that lies behind the face you look at.'

FOR REFLECTION

1. Do you learn about God through other people?
2. Can you think of people who have helped you understand God better? What was the particular way they helped?
3. Do you look at other people on buses or trains and wonder what their story is, or do you fail even to notice them?
4. When did you last ask someone you live with, what it is like being them?

PRAYER

Father, what must you be like who can create so many different things and people, and yet manifest yourself through each of them? I thank you for all whom you have put into my life. Many I did not choose, but you chose them. Give me your eyes to see them as you do. What a difference that would make to me.

I ask with confidence because I ask this in the name of your Son. Amen.

Hearing God through Life's Hurts

———◆———

FROM THE KITCHEN Elizabeth heard the key turn in the front door. This was the moment that she had been dreading ever since Michael, her husband, had phoned her, shortly after 3 o'clock to tell her that he had been made redundant. It was not a bolt out of the blue, for three weeks ago it had been put out that there were going to be drastic cut backs in the firm. Michael had then sunk into a deep gloom and had been going backwards and forwards between fear and anxiety, and then anger and resentment. 'Why did God seem to have it in for them?', was the question he kept asking. Elizabeth did not know how to answer that, for it was true, they were having quite a run of difficulties. Their first born, a little boy, had been dead on birth. That had been just over two years ago. Michael had been shattered by that, and then when Debby arrived, she obviously was not a healthy child and gave them both much anxiety, but clearly Michael continued to grieve that he had lost his son.

They were both Catholics, though Elizabeth was the stronger of the two. She had tried to comfort Michael and had talked to him about accepting God's will and there was a need to 'carry one's cross'. Michael's answer had always been, 'But why pick on us?', and

Elizabeth did not know the answer to that. And that is why she dreaded having to face him now that the worst had happened.

He looked so vulnerable and crushed, standing there in the hall. She went to him and held him close. It was a relief that he allowed her to do this and nothing was said.

Thoughts raced through Elizabeth's mind as she stood there with her arms around her husband. 'Why, Lord, did you not hear our prayers? What about those Masses I attended ever since we heard of the threat of redundancy?' What of all those prayers, said here and there as she had gone about her daily chores?

Father Smith, their parish priest, had preached a beautiful sermon only last Sunday on the love of God. It had been quite moving, but now it all seemed like hot air. Both Elizabeth and Michael had turned to this loving God in their trouble and he had not answered their cry for help. Elizabeth grew cold and her mind seemed to suddenly sweat with fear as she saw where her thoughts were leading her. 'My God! What would they do if she ceased to believe?' She had always felt, somehow, that it was right to believe in God and Christianity and all that. She had grown up with the idea that God was good and that he could be trusted and that if you asked his help he would 'hear your prayer'. All that now looked very shallow, untrue, yes even superstitious. Perhaps it was all a con.

Michael broke in on these thoughts saying, 'But why? Why? Why?', and they both wept there standing in the hall.

It was old Alice Micklethorpe who gave the first glimmer of hope a few days later. She heard of the bad news, had donned her hat, coat and gloves and come round to comfort the young couple.

'Don't be silly, deary, God never sends troubles. Troubles come from all sorts of places, but never from the good God. Deary me – what a thought!', and she shook her old head causing her double chin to wobble. 'This great God of ours, somehow permits bad things to happen', and she rolled her tired eyes as though it pained her to think such a thought, 'but he never causes them', and she was quite emphatic over that. 'What a terrible day it is for caterpillars when they start to become butterflies. They nearly cease to be. They are stripped of everything they had and have to lie tied up in a cocoon-like pod for weeks. But, look what happens in the end.' And again the chins swayed back and forth as though to add weight to her words.

'Was this God's answer to all those prayers', thought Elizabeth, because from then on Michael began to grow calm. It was not a sudden release, but at least there was a glimmer. Nothing was actually said, but when Alice got up to leave after giving her words of wisdom, Michael hugged her.

He called the people and his disciples to him and said, 'If anyone wants to be a follower of mine, let him renounce himself and take up his cross and follow me. Anyone who wants to save his life will lose it; but anyone who loses his life for my sake, and for the sake of the gospel, will save it. What gain, then, is it for anyone to win the whole world and forfeit his life? And indeed what can anyone offer in exchange for his life? For if anyone in this sinful and adulterous generation is ashamed of me and of my words, the Son of man will also be ashamed of him when he comes in the glory of his Father with the holy angels.'
(Mark 8:34–38)

When tragedies hit us, it is very hard to believe in the love of God. Times of prayer become very difficult because we are wondering just how God could let something like this happen to us. Deep down we feel a resentment, and yet at the same time we feel guilty about not wanting what has happened and feel a bit small in arguing against God. The trouble is that we know he is always right and somehow it does not seem fair.

All sorts of problems can arise from this. Either we decide to continue with God, but our attitude becomes one of suspicion and fear, and we will not want to go very deep with him, or we will decide to drop him completely and go our own way.

Elizabeth and Michael had obviously been taught the necessity of carrying their crosses, but exactly what that meant had not been made clear to them. They mistakenly thought every hardship that came their way had to be willingly embraced as God's will.

I think many of us, like Elizabeth and Michael, have received bad teaching about the will of God. We've all been told, 'This is your cross' or 'It is God's will', but is that always true? We must not call all suffering the 'cross', because the 'cross' is any suffering that comes *because* we have decided to follow the Lord. See in the biblical passage that Jesus says *if* anyone *wants* be a disciple then he (or she) will have to suffer certain things. This does not mean that other sufferings cannot be used meritoriously, but we should not call them the 'cross'.

I believe there is an important difference between God's will and God's permissive will (i.e. what God *allows* to happen). I don't believe God willed that Michael should be made redundant, lose his little son and have a daughter with ill health. It is true, God could have prevented these things, but he seems to allow them because he sees how these very evils can be used to produce growth and good. Because Michael thought of God as sending him all these trials, he felt a deep resentment and hostility towards God; he was reluctant to simply accept these things and offer them up. But once Alice's idea of God being on his side took root in him, there started a new growth, which might never have begun if he had not suffered in the first place.

We have no abiding city here. We were not made to be here forever, and we have got it wrong if we think we have a right to a trouble-free existence on earth. Sin has thrown everything out of balance, but God can use these imbalances to produce patience, love, understanding and gentleness.

Honest and genuine prayer must involve expressing our hurt and questions to God. He is big enough to cope with them, and we often grow most as Christians through our response to setbacks and suffering. We clearly should not look for hardship, but when it comes it *can* be used for good.

FOR REFLECTION

1. Do you see misfortune as God's will for you?
2. Do you ever express your deeper feelings to God or do you feel that would be wrong?
3. Can you see the difference between carrying your cross and bearing ordinary suffering?

PRAYER

Lord, I want to trust my life and all that I have into your care. Forgive me, for I have often doubted your love, I have feared that you would take from me everything that means most to me. But, Lord, that is how I learnt about you. Forgive us all for our blindness. Amen.

Hearing God through Weakness

—◆—

'WHY DOES GOD make it so difficult to know him? Why can't he just appear to us, or do something staggering and make everyone believe? Why has he got to hide, to make things obscure? Why does he allow us, his creatures, almost to be able to prove that he does not exist? Why does he sit up in heaven and never move a muscle to prove people wrong?'

These thoughts and many other angry ones were buzzing through Jeremy's mind as he walked home after his evening visit with Paul to the local pub. They met there most evenings and they had become good friends. Jeremy was a believer, Paul was not.

That evening Paul had been dismantling all Jeremy's arguments for God's existence. It was not that Paul was out to destroy Jeremy's faith, he really was just sharing his views and honest doubts. The trouble was they were very convincing. He argued that with the advance of science and knowledge all the reasons why primitive people believed in a god had now been proved false. Thunder and lightening were not signs of a mighty god storming around the heavens, they could all be explained scientifically. 'You see, Jeremy, we just do not need to have a god to explain all these mysteries. All that once argued for the existence of a god has now been uncovered.' Jeremy could see the logic behind this reasoning, but deep down he knew it was not the last word. What annoyed him was he could not find the last word.

On his way home, Jeremy found angry thoughts rising up within him. If he had been ruthlessly honest with himself, he would have admitted that for a moment he had touched the first glimmerings of a thought that perhaps all that he held dear and important might suddenly be proved to be false. Such a thought was immediately expelled – but it had been there and Jeremy somehow knew it.

'Why can't you manifest yourself?' It was as though he shouted that to the skies. Only this morning at Mass, the reading had begun, 'Oh, that you would tear the heavens open and come down' (Isaiah 64:1). 'Why sit up there, and let your creatures disprove your existence? You are meant to be a strong God full of power and glory. Why don't you do something? Is it that you cannot? Or is it that you do not really exist?' There, he had actually said the words for the moment Jeremy's world tottered and swayed, 'O God, what if . . .?'

❖

There he [Elijah] went into a cave and spent the night there. Then the word of Yahweh came to him saying, 'What are you doing here, Elijah?' He replied, 'I am full of jealous zeal for Yahweh Sabaoth, because the Israelites have abandoned your covenant, have torn down your altars and put your prophets to the sword. I am the only one left, and now they want to kill me.' Then he was told, 'Go out and stand on the mountain before Yahweh.' For at that moment Yahweh was going by. A mighty hurricane split the mountains and shattered the rocks before Yahweh. But Yahweh was not in the hurricane. And after the hurricane, an earthquake. But Yahweh was not in the earthquake. And

*after the earthquake, fire. But Yahweh was not in the
fire. And after the fire, a light murmuring sound. And
when Elijah heard this, he covered his face with his
cloak and went out and stood at the entrance of the
cave. Then a voice came to him, which said, 'What
are you doing here, Elijah?' He replied, 'I am full of
jealous zeal for Yahweh, God Sabaoth, because the
Israelites have abandoned your covenant, have torn
down your altars and put your prophets to the sword.
I am the only one left and now they want to kill me.'
'Go,' Yahweh said, 'go back by the same way to the
desert of Damascus. You must go and anoint Hazael
as king of Aram.'*

(1 Kings 19:9–15)

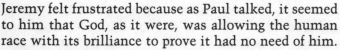

Jeremy felt frustrated because as Paul talked, it seemed
to him that God, as it were, was allowing the human
race with its brilliance to prove it had no need of him.

Jeremy believed that God existed, but he seemed
quite unable to give arguments to support his convic-
tion. Paul, on the other hand, was showing how primitive people had needed something to explain what they
saw in the universe; science had now provided the
answers and God was not needed as an explanation.
Deep down Jeremy had to concede that God had done
himself out of a job, by letting the human mind
develop so well in its understanding of the universe.
It seemed now, that God had very little to commend
him. What could Jeremy say in the face of all this?
That was why he felt frustrated on his way home and
he began wishing that God would stop hiding himself
and come out and do something mind-blowing.

I am sure we have all wrestled with the question,
why does God apparently hide? The very power and
splendour of the universe convinced early civilisations,

that God existed, but now science claims to be able to explain the wonders of the world.

In the passage from the book of Kings, God is showing us that he does not always reveal himself in might and dazzling power but that he can come in hiddenness and gentleness. It was not in the hurricane or the earthquake or the fire that he came to Elijah, but in a soft breeze.

Jesus, who told us that to see him was to see the Father, conquered Satan, not in the clashing of swords or with stupendous demonstrations of power, but by allowing himself to be seemingly defeated. He appeared to have downed his weapons and offered no resistance – he was 'like a lamb led to the slaughter house' (Isaiah 53:7). It is the strange story of victory through apparent weakness, summer following winter, death being followed by rising.

God so loved the world that he sent his Son into it. He was not born into a royal or powerful family; he did not become a Roman. He chose to belong to a poor nation, quite small and occupied by a foreign power. He chose to be a nobody, an unprivileged person, someone who could be done away with without anyone raising a voice in protest. He came to share in our human weakness.

> Who, being in the form of God,
> did not count equality with God
> something to be grasped.
> But he emptied himself,
> taking the form of a slave,
> becoming as human beings are.
>
> (Philippians 2:6–7)

We tend to think of God in terms of glory, power, splendour, and while all that is true it is not the whole picture, there is another side to him. He came among us in weakness.

It is only through prayer that we can come to know both the power and the weakness of God. He wishes to encourage us when we feel confused, bewildered as to why he, who has all power, does not act in some powerful way to convince this unbelieving world. His ways are not our ways, and he can draw his purposes out of very unlikely situations. Things that seem to us useless, even disasters, he can use and make life giving. I am sure we all know stories in which what seemed totally hopeless, in the end, becomes a source of blessing.

In prayer, we may have to wrestle with God. We read in Genesis 32 that Jacob wrestled with him and limped for ever afterwards. It is not wrong to ask God questions. We will not get immediate answers. Personally, I find it often takes quite a long time before I see what I am looking for. The answer may come in something someone says, or I may read it in a book, or an idea comes into my mind. God does speak to us but not in voices from heaven, at least I do not hear him that way. Prayer is a relationship and if you treat it as such, you will find God does teach you. You will learn about God, gain new insights, find answers to difficult questions, and gradually you will find you are beginning to know something of this God of ours, who can come to us in powerful storms or great winds or in gentle breezes, 'who visits us like the dawn from on high' (from the Benedictus).

FOR REFLECTION

1. What is your reaction when you see Jesus being scourged, ill treated, and crucified and he does not defend himself?
2. Can you accept God when he does not show signs that he is present and he allows his creatures to all but prove that he does not exist.

3. Which do you prefer, the God who came down at Elijah's bidding and consummed the sacrifice with fire (see 1 Kings 18:20–40) or the God who waits patiently and refuses to blow people's minds?
4. Have you ever felt helpless in trying to tell others about God? Did this discourage you or could you find strength in your weakness?

PRAYER

Lord, you are certainly not like us. Even my best ideas of you are not you. How can I know you unless you come and teach me yourself. You have sent me your Holy Spirit to do just that. Spirit of the living God I ask you to show me the Lord. Grant to me an understanding that does not come from reasoning, just show me the Lord. Amen.

Praying through the Spirit

◄——►

IMAGINE a very small island, set far out in the Pacific Ocean, a long way from any land mass or other island, lying somewhere between latitude 20 and 30 degrees south of the equator. At most its length would be just over 3 miles and at its widest it is just under 1 mile. The island is very rocky and that could explain why humans never seem to have settled there. When I say it is rocky. I do not mean you to imagine a solid rock mass, bare and forbidding in the hot sun, rather it is covered in rocky outcrops, and soil between the rocks is poor and does not go very deep. In this soil all sorts of plants grow and many of them have beautiful flowers. At the north end of the island, where the widest part lies, there are a few trees.

The island supports a number of animals and insects. You can find lizards, snakes, rodents, and of course many birds. The main inhabitant is the turtle. Rather strange to say, there are butterflies on the island, but for some unknown reason they have never learnt to fly. They have wings, in fact they are quite large and they are of beautiful colours. Often you will see them sitting on the rocks displaying these iridescent colours to any who would care to admire them. But, while these butterflies may be very beautiful, life is not that easy for them. When they climb up the stalks of the flowers to get at the nectar and pollen, the great sails on their backs become quite a problem, especially when the plants are growing close together. The real difficulty starts when they try to come down. They have to come down backwards and this means that the wings get hopelessly entangled with awkward stems criss-crossing in the mass of vegetation. But, then, life has its problems, and so they have learnt to live with them.

One day there was an immense storm and every living thing had to seek shelter somewhere on the island. Under every rock and stone, you could have found some small, or not so small, creature sheltering for its life. The wind blew, and the rain came down in buckets and it lasted for most of the day. When finally it had blown itself out and the sun came out to dry up the soaked island, all the small creatures came out to see what was left of their homes.

Soon news travelled round that something interesting had been found. In the north part of the island there was a very drenched butterfly, obviously blown there from some far off land, and the exciting thing was that this butterfly could fly.

It was Tommy Toad who found her. He knew straight away that she was not from the island, for her wings were rather shabby and were not highly coloured as the other butterflies.

'How have you come here? I do not recall ever seeing you before.'

'I was flying when a great storm arose and before I could get to my home I was blown out to sea. From then on I do not remember much until I opened my eyes not long ago. Can you tell me where I am?', she said rather sadly.

'You are not far from Turtle Cove,' Tommy replied, 'but what is all this about flying? Here the butterflies do not fly.'

'They don't fly', she answered incredulously. 'But

that is what wings are for.' And she opened her wings to allow the sun to dry them. After a few moments she flew up into the air to demonstrate to Tommy who sat there with his eyes bulging with astonishment.

'Wait here', said Tommy and he rushed off to assemble as many of the island's butterflies as he could find.

It did not take very long to gather a large crowd for the island was small and news travelled quickly. Tommy addressed the assembled crowd and was obviously very proud of his find. After the necessary introductions the little butterfly demonstrated the art of flying while the crowd gasped and ooed.

'So that's what they are for. Why didn't someone tell us?' The excitement was intense and some of the younger butterflies immediately began to try their skill at flying, but not having very strong muscles, nor being well versed in aeronautics, there were accidents. The older and so-called wiser ones, went round the island shaking their heads saying: 'It is all very dangerous.'

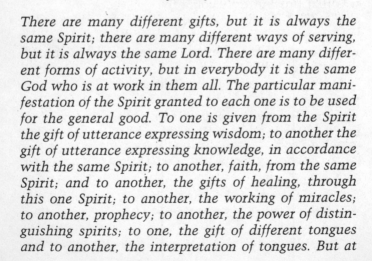

There are many different gifts, but it is always the same Spirit; there are many different ways of serving, but it is always the same Lord. There are many different forms of activity, but in everybody it is the same God who is at work in them all. The particular manifestation of the Spirit granted to each one is to be used for the general good. To one is given from the Spirit the gift of utterance expressing wisdom; to another the gift of utterance expressing knowledge, in accordance with the same Spirit; to another, faith, from the same Spirit; and to another, the gifts of healing, through this one Spirit; to another, the working of miracles; to another, prophecy; to another, the power of distinguishing spirits; to one, the gift of different tongues and to another, the interpretation of tongues. But at

*work in all these is one and the same Spirit, distribut-
ing them at will to each individual.*

(1 Corinthians 12:4–11)

◆━━━◆

When I studied theology, we cannot have spent much
time on the gifts of the Holy Spirit because I cannot
recall anything about them. The general opinion at
that time seemed to be that these gifts were only given
to the Church at the beginning so, as it were, to give
it a boost.

Since Vatican II we know that this is not the case.
In the Document on the Church (section 12) it says
that the gifts of the Holy Spirit belong to the whole
Church, they are not reserved for the clergy alone, and
they are to be received with gratitude. In the passage
from 1 Corinthians, Paul lists the gifts of the Spirit;
we are not concerned with them all here, but there are
books written which deal specifically with them, or
there are wise people in the church who can help us
explore them further.

Rather like the butterflies who had never used their
wings, we, who have never been instructed in the gifts,
have not known quite how to allow them to operate.
Mistakes have been made, and, sadly, the charisms (as
they are sometimes called) are now often viewed with
suspicion.

The gifts of the Holy Spirit belong to the Holy Spirit
and can be lent to any believer 'for the general good'
(1 Corinthians 12:7). They are gifts for service and any
member of the church can be used by the Holy Spirit
for the Spirit's purpose. It is wrong to think that these
gifts are only confined to people in the charismatic
renewal. The object of the renewal is precisely to
restore the gifts to the whole church.

So what about praying in the Spirit? How can we let
the Spirit speak to us? I think it is helpful to see human

beings in terms of body, soul and spirit (although, of
course, we should be a little wary of categorising things
too simply). Through the body we are 'physical' beings
and partake in the material world. Through the soul
we are 'rational' beings, able to live in the immaterial
as well as the material world and bringing into play our
reason, our will, our imagination and our emotions.
Through the spirit we are 'spiritual' beings and operate
in a realm beyond the reach of body and soul. It is
through our spirit that God communicates with us by
his Spirit. 'The Spirit himself joins with our spirit to
bear witness that we are children of God' (Romans
8:16).

We can learn about God through our intellects. We
are taught the truths about God, but these truths can
be just information, facts; they need to become bearers
of life. This is the work of the Holy Spirit. He can take
what we learn through our minds and make it life-
giving or he can impart life-giving knowledge directly
through our spirits into our minds – this we call inspiration. God promised that he would lead us into truth
this way.

> but the Paraclete, the Holy Spirit,
> whom the Father will send in my name,
> will teach you everything
> and remind you of all I have said to you.
>
> (John 14:26)

In the western world we rely heavily on receiving
knowledge through our reason and intellect. We are
logical, scientific. In our times, the Holy Spirit is being
rediscovered, but many of us are in danger of being too
cerebral; we are suspicious of inspiration, of dreams,
of inner enlightenments. I believe it is right for the
Church to be cautious about inner promptings as there
are plenty of nutcases around who imagine every
prompting must be the Holy Spirit. Satan can manifest

himself as an angel of light, and care must be taken that we are not led astray. What we most need is discernment (referred to in Paul's list as the 'power of distinguishing spirits'). We need to discern which spirit is at work – the Holy Spirit, the human spirit or an evil spirit?

When we pray we can use our bodies to help us. Posture and gestures can both be employed. We can use our imaginations, our minds, our memories. But God can also use our spirits, and when he does so, he bypasses our body and reasoning process, and goes directly to our spirit. We cannot cause this to happen – it is God's work and he knows when to do it. I see this as the beginning of contemplation. I don't think contemplation is about having great illuminations or visions or hearing voices. It seems at first to be a great darkness for God is not communicating with us through our reason but through our spirit. It is God's gift to us and hence not something we should actively seek.

The gifts of the Spirit that St Paul writes about also operate in this realm of the spirit. I believe much teaching is needed about these gifts if they are to be used rightly. One of the gifts mentioned is that of wisdom, and an example of this is when we receive insights from God to help us in a given situation – perhaps to help us counsel another person. We seem to receive from beyond ourselves the right words to say, or perhaps we receive a particular insight which gives us new understanding.

I don't think the gift of tongues (the last on Paul's list) is such a weird gift as many people imagine. We have had very little teaching about it in the Catholic Church and perhaps that explains the mystery surrounding it. I am sure we all recognise that there are times in prayer when we simply do not have the words to express ourselves. It could be a time of great consolation or desolation – both experiences can reduce us to silence. The gift of tongues operates when the Holy Spirit begins to pray through people. Unintelligible words, what seems like a foreign language, sounds with no apparent meaning come out, but I believe that at a deeper level this prayer does have meaning even if our minds cannot grasp it. 'The Spirit too comes to help us in our weakness, for, when we do not know how to pray properly, then the Spirit personally makes our petitions for us in groans that cannot be put into words; and he who sees into all hearts knows what the Spirit means because the prayers that the Spirit makes for God's holy people are always in accordance with the mind of God.' (Romans 8:26,27)

As I say, this is a complex area and one that needs much more exploration than I can give here. If we are going to take prayer seriously, we will need to find a wise guide to help us move into the realm of praying in the Spirit.

FOR REFLECTION

1. When you pray, who do you talk to? The Father, Jesus or the Holy Spirit?
2. Why do you think the Holy Spirit gets neglected?
3. Do you know the difference between the gifts of the Holy Spirit and the fruit of the Holy Spirit? (See 1 Corinthians 12:4–11 and Galatians 5:22–26.)
4. We have received the Holy Spirit in many different ways, so we can all say 'we have got the Holy Spirit'. The real question is 'Has the Holy Spirit got us?' Has he got you?

PRAYER

Holy Spirit of God. Forgive me for neglecting you so often. You are the one who always talks about the

Father and Jesus. Please talk to me about them so that
I begin to know them and not just know about them.
You were sent to me for this very reason; please, I
invite you to teach me. Amen.

Two Ways of Asking

◆━━◆

ELEANOR'S HEART SANK when she saw from her notebook that number 27 Snellgrove Road was her next port of call. Eleanor was a home help, and Eileen Grindmore, to whom she was now going, was a very demanding person. Eileen was confined to a wheelchair, and had been for some years, but she always had long lists of requests when Eleanor went to visit. Eleanor found the constant demands quite exhausting.

'I've been waiting for you all morning', were the words that greeted Eleanor as she entered the house with a somewhat heavy heart. 'I want you to pop down to the corner shop and get me some string, some ribbons, and some Christmas wrapping paper. We've got to get these presents wrapped and ready, for there is now not much time left.'

'I also want some bread, and would you look and see if there is any fruit in the larder? I shall also want you to phone Mrs Rye and ask her to be sure that she calls in here after she has collected her daughter from school.' And so it went on, one request after another. Eleanor knew that poor Mrs Grindmore was severely handicapped and that she depended upon someone to help her, but in some way Eleanor felt she was just an object to be used.

Annie Punch was very different. She was also handicapped and confined to a wheelchair, but, somehow

Eleanor, though she would work just as hard for her, looked forward to those visits. On arrival Eleanor would be made to sit down and tell Mrs Punch all that had happened since her last visit. She wanted to know everything and she seemed to have a very good memory, and remembered to ask about this and that. It was only in the course of conversation that requests would appear. 'I've bought a few Christmas presents and I have tried parcelling them up, and they look a real mess, I wonder . . .' and she would give that rather helpless look which said, 'I really am not much use, and it pains me to be like that. Forgive me for needing someone like you.' Those words were not said, but what was communicated was, 'I cannot do it, but that is how things are and I accept them'. Of course, Eleanor was only too delighted to take the crinkled heap that was on the table and unwrap it, straighten out the paper and make a new parcel.

Eleanor often wondered what the difference was between these two handicapped people. Maybe it was that Mrs Punch rarely asked for anything just for herself; and yet Mrs Grindmore also had parcels for other people. Was it the way in which Mrs Punch asked that was so different? Mrs Grindmore seemed to be giving orders, whereas Mrs Punch seemed to make the request out of her helplessness, and yet there was no sense of seeking pity or sympathy.

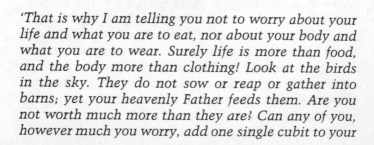

'*That is why I am telling you not to worry about your life and what you are to eat, nor about your body and what you are to wear. Surely life is more than food, and the body more than clothing! Look at the birds in the sky. They do not sow or reap or gather into barns; yet your heavenly Father feeds them. Are you not worth much more than they are? Can any of you, however much you worry, add one single cubit to your*

span of life? And why worry about clothing? Think of the flowers growing in the fields; they never have to work or spin; yet I assure you that not even Solomon in all his royal robes was clothed like one of these. Now if that is how God clothes the wild flowers growing in the field which are there today and thrown into the furnace tomorrow, will he not much more look after you, you who have so little faith? So do not worry; do not say, "What are we to eat? What are we to drink? What are we to wear?" It is the gentiles who set their hearts on all these things. Your heavenly Father knows you need them all. Set your hearts on his kingdom first, and on God's saving justice, and all these other things will be given you as well. So do not worry about tomorrow: tomorrow will take care of itself. Each day has enough trouble of its own.'

(Matthew 6:25–34)

I imagine that most of us learnt about prayer as asking God for our needs. We ask him to bless our mother and father, our brothers and sisters. We also thank him for the good things we have received and ask for his protection. I can remember tacking onto the family list, friends and relatives until the list became a long litany. I had dreadful problems pruning it. I felt guilty if I left someone out and feared some terrible thing would happen to them. What odd creatures we are. I know someone who for years prayed for 'the woman who fell out of the train'. He had read this in the paper and had felt compassion for the poor soul, so she got tucked into the family list. We can learn to rattle through these lists without paying attention, and my friend told me that years after reading about this poor woman, he discovered that he was still mentioning her in his automatic list.

Many of us need to realise that there is much more

to prayer than petition. In the passage from Matthew, God is asking us what our priorities are. Are we too concerned with our own wants and wishes? Jesus tells us that if we spent more time seeking the kingdom of God, then many of our requests would actually get attended to without us bothering about them. But what does it mean to seek the kingdom of God? Many people think that the kingdom of God refers to heaven, but if this is so, how can we seek the kingdom through prayer?

I think, instead, we should see the kingdom of God as wherever God is obeyed, wherever God is accepted to be in charge. To seek the kingdom of God is to search into our lives and see if we are allowing God to have his way.

To obey God is to accept his Son. Most of us would think that to obey God means following his commandments. While, this is of course true, the following of God's commandments comes second to accepting the gift of his Son. In John's Gospel, Jesus tells us what obeying the Father means: 'This is carrying out God's work: you must believe in the one he has sent.' (John 6:29)

So, when we pray we need to acknowledge to the Father that we believe in and accept his son. We thank him for this wonderful gift, we ask his pardon that we did not accept Jesus when he lived on earth, but hounded him out of the city and hung him on a cross. We bless the Father for taking this terrible act of ours and using it for his purposes. Time and time again we tell the Father that we accept all that he has done for us in his son. We thank him that through Christ, sins are forgiven, that we can live a new life as God's children. This is to seek the kingdom of God. We ask that what the Father has achieved may have its full effect in us and in the world.

Many of the prayers said in church express all these

truths, but because these truths have not yet become ours we can tend to mouth the words and not grasp the full meaning. For example, we can call our Lord our saviour, but do we act as though he is our saviour? Say, for example, that we were told that we would be dead next week, where would we put our hope? Would it be in a list of good things we have done? Or would we immediately say: 'My hope and trust are in the merits of Jesus Christ'?

So how do we see prayer? Do we view it as a series of requests we present to God? As a list of people we have promised to pray for? Or, as in Eleanor's relationship with Mrs Punch, is it more of a conversation, a real relating? The Scripture passage is showing us that petitions should not be our priority in prayer. Naturally, we want to tell God our needs but there is something wrong if they dominate the relationship. There is much more to life and to prayer than petition and worrying about our own wants and wishes. The passage is not telling us just to sit around expecting God to feed and clothe us. The Lord is saying, 'Seek the kingdom first, and then attend to your needs'. To seek the kingdom is to want Jesus Christ to take his rightful place as Lord and master of this earth. He himself told us that all power and all authority had been given to him; we invite him to exercise that power and authority, beginning in our own lives.

FOR REFLECTION

1. What are your priorities in prayer? Do petitions dominate?
2. If they do dominate, what does that show about your image of God?
3. What do you think it means to 'set your heart on the kingdom first'? How might that affect your own life and the way you pray?

PRAYER

Father God you know my needs and you know how much they mean to me. Do not let me become so immersed in my wants that I forget your wants. I thank you that you are loving and you know and understand how things are with me. Teach me about your kingdom, heal me of my blindness. May your Spirit teach me that I belong to you and you belong to me. Thank you for being you. Amen.

Unanswered Prayer

◆══◆

HIS NAME IS XU GUOMING. I have no idea how one pronounces it, and that has proved a problem because I undertook to pray for him.

I first saw his photo on the front page of a newspaper. Beside the photo, in large letters, was the heading:

FIRST PROTESTERS SENTENCED TO DEATH IN CHINA.

My friend, and I feel I can now call him that, looked so young and alone, and I suppose it was just that which caught my mind – or was it my heart? It was a head and shoulders photo, and although his head was slightly bowed, his eyes were raised and looking straight in front of him. Whether he was looking at the person reading his death sentence, I do not know, but I do know that the drama of that moment was communicated to me. On his left was the face of a soldier, also young, but the peak of his military cap was pulled well down over his face and all that I could see was his mouth, which was stern and set.

I wondered what it must be like to hear a sentence of death being passed on you. I could imagine my own fear and panic, and I wanted to stretch out to this unknown stranger from the other side of the world. It was then that I undertook to pray for him.

I cut the photo out and pasted it on my cupboard

door to make sure that I would not forget him. I felt a bit ashamed at doing this. Surely I would remember this young man and his trouble without having to put his picture on my door? But I went ahead and his picture is still there.

I prayed and prayed that God would spare him from the sentence passed. I prayed anywhere I could – while shopping, as I walked from one place to another. I was somewhat encouraged when after a few days I read in the papers that various heads of government had sent messages asking for leniency. I was hopeful that these requests might be listened to.

It must have been ten days after first noticing his picture in the papers, that I saw on television that the death sentence had been carried out. I was watching the news one evening and they announced that three young people had been executed, and I saw some shots taken of the three men being marched into a vast public hall to be executed in front of a large, silent crowd. Thank God we were spared seeing the execution, but I did see my friend just for a moment and that picture still haunts me. I can remember trying to comfort myself by saying: 'Well, he is dead now. He does not have to fear it anymore. It is over.' All I could do now was to commend him to God.

Had my prayers failed? Did I not pray enough? Should I have asked others to pray? Did God not hear me? Why should he hear me, a westerner, someone living a comfortable and maybe compromised life? A veritable storm was let loose in me and all sorts of frightening questions burst into my mind.

◆━━━◆

'So I say to you: Ask, and it will be given to you; search, and you will find; knock, and the door will be opened to you. For everyone who asks receives; everyone who searches finds; everyone who knocks

*will have the door opened. What father among you, if
his son asked for a fish would hand him a snake? Or
if he asked for an egg, hand him a scorpion? If you
then, evil as you are, know how to give your children
what is good, how much more will the heavenly
Father give the Holy Spirit to those who ask him!'*

(Luke 11:9–13)

◄━━━━━►

What does this passage from St Luke mean? Is it really
saying that God will grant all our requests? Why then
did my young Chinese friend die when I was praying
so hard for him? I don't know the answer to that question, but I do know that many of us, myself included,
have faulty pictures of God and we need to let these
be changed in the light of Jesus' life, death and resurrection. Perhaps we will then see that God's purposes are
different from ours and that we need to trust him
more. Perhaps we will see that he *does* answer our
prayers, but in ways we would not expect or cannot
fully understand in this life. If, as Jesus says in the
above passage, God gives good things to his children,
mustn't it be true that God's ways are more than we
can comprehend and our images of him are often inad-
equate?

My own pictures of God have undergone, and are
still undergoing, transformation. I grew up understanding him to be almighty and powerful, I imagined that
he conquered evil by blowing it out of existence by
force. Over quite a number of years now I have begun
to understand that God often seems to deal with evil
through apparent weakness. When Jesus started his
public life, he did miracles, cured the sick, raised the
dead. In other words he seemed to come against Satan
with power and strength. But after the transfiguration
he seemed to change. He now talked about going to
Jerusalem and dying.

On Mount Tabor, Moses and Elijah appeared with him and we are told that they were talking about 'his passing'. Was Jesus then receiving clearer instruction from his Father about the Father's way of defeating Satan? After this encounter on the mount, Jesus was different. He did fewer miracles and he set his face like flint to go to Jerusalem. He began to refer more and more to his death and resurrection, and his disciples did not know what he was talking about.

Jesus could have conquered Satan at a moment's notice, but it seemed the Father was going to defeat Satan by apparently allowing him to conquer his Son. Jesus permitted the evil one to do his damnedest against him. But having died, having allowed the worst to happen, Jesus was called back by the Father from the kingdom of darkness and thus through weakness Jesus overcame. He calls us to follow him. It seems that he is asking us to trust that he can turn even what appears to us a disaster into something from which good can come. He is our Father, he loves us and wants the best for us. Who can tell how he used my prayers, and no doubt the prayers of many others, for some good purpose? True, the young man died, but life here on earth is not our final aim.

I believe God to be good and I feel content to allow my friend to fall into his hands. At Mass we pray for the departed and after mentioning our 'brothers and sisters', meaning all Christians no matter what denomination, we add 'and all those who have left this world in your friendship'. That is a fairly wide-ranging prayer. Many people may well be in God's friendship without actually knowing God personally. This does not mean that I deny that no one can come to the Father save through Jesus Christ; it is still through Christ that we all go to the Father, but God is the judge and not us. That is why I love the Church's care for everyone, no matter who they are.

If we judge things according to this life alone, we will find many things to lament and regret. But we need to remember that we were not made just for this life. Our prayers may seem unanswered now but we do not always see things as God sees them, and much of the Christian journey is about learning to trust him even when things look desperate and he appears to have abandoned us.

FOR REFLECTION

1. How do you judge things? Is it from the viewpoint of this life or from the viewpoint of eternity?
2. How do you react to upsets in life and to times when your prayers seem to go unanswered?
3. What are the things that you pray about?
4. Can you really trust God?

PRAYER

Lord, from where I stand I see many needs and wants. You have promised that if we ask you would answer.

I do find it very difficult to see how you answer some of my prayers. I know you are not bound to answer my prayers in the way I would like you to do, but at times it really does look as though you did not hear me.

Forgive me for talking to you in this way, but I want you to be a God I can say anything to. Thank you for not being touchy. I offer you my mind and ask you to enlighten me. I am sure that is what you want. Amen.

When Prayer becomes Difficult

◆━━➤

IT WAS SOME YEARS now since Ronald had made the retreat that so changed his life. Jane, his wife, had suggested that as the family were all but off their hands, they should go for the last few days of Holy Week to an abbey not too far from where they lived. Ronald, who would not have called himself a religious type, though he had remained loyal to the practice of his faith, thought the idea was good and it seemed a fine thing to do.

There was nothing very outstanding about the retreat, most of the participants thought it was helpful, nice, pleasant, but for Ronald it was life changing. Truths, which he had known and thought he had accepted, suddenly took on a new and staggering meaning. Quite simply, Ronald had met God in all his wonder, mercy and love. The outcome of the retreat was that Ronald began to read Scripture and to pray. He decided to give up a quarter of an hour of his lunch break and spent it in a church quite close to his office in the heart of the city.

Prayer, became a new experience. Before he had mumbled prayers asking God to bless his family, his work, and, in times of tension or crisis, he allowed this prayer time to be lengthened a little. He could see that there was quite a lot of self in those prayers, everything was rather geared to what he wanted and God was seen as the 'wealthy one' who could provide if stroked nicely. He could even see quite a bit of superstition in the way he used to think. What held him now was the fact that God was good. He did not have to win his favour. The incredible thing was that God loved Ronald, he loved everyone and he wanted to be loved in return. Ronald found that his prayer became God centred, God was no longer seen for what he could do for Ronald. What had seized hold of Ronald's mind was that before he had made any response to God's love, God had sent his Son to die for his sins and had risen from death and wanted to live in Ronald and help him live for God and not for himself. This fact bowled Ronald over; it was not a calculating love, it was not tit for tat, it was totally generous.

For several months after that retreat during his prayer time he kept coming back to these truths, which he had listened to many times, but somehow had not really heard. He pondered over them and never seemed to tire of them.

Soon questions began to rise up from all this pondering and these led him to books. There were some at the back of the church where he prayed, but they were few in number. He noticed a small notice giving the address of the shop that supplied them. He now began to buy books and to read. He found that he was really quite ignorant about the truths of his faith. The problem he found in the book shop was that there were so many books and they all seemed to be exactly what he ought to read, though he soon discovered that not all of them lived up to their promise. Fortunately, Mr Dart, who served in the shop, was widely read and his advice proved of immense help.

But all this was, as it were, in the past. Ronald was now beginning to experience this time of prayer as burdensome. He certainly was not so faithful to the fifteen minutes and at the least provocation he was ready to arrive late or go early. Somehow the time had lost its freshness and the ideas, which had so held his mind, no longer had their appeal. Also he was full of distractions and it seemed as if God had gone away, and the fifteen minutes, once not long enough, now seemed interminable. The temptation was to skip this time of prayer. He was getting nothing from it, in fact he seemed to become more and more irritable, clearly it was no good going on flogging a dead horse. He also found that the books he had turned to had lost their interest, and the train journey home was now spent with the evening paper.

This state of things went on for some time, and while Ronald did make some gallant efforts to keep up his prayer, he felt he was fighting a losing battle, then one day when he went to the church during his lunch hour he found a mission was in progress. He had only just walked in when he heard the priest say: 'When you no longer get anything out of prayer, you are on the brink of learning how to pray'. Ronald made enquiries and found out who the priest was and he made an appointment with him. Ronald had found a spiritual director who could begin to explain to him just what was happening in his spiritual life.

Now when I came to you, brothers, I did not come with any brilliance of oratory or wise argument to announce to you the mystery of God. I was resolved that the only knowledge I would have while I was with you was knowledge of Jesus, and of him as the crucified Christ. I came among you in weakness, in fear and great trembling and what I spoke and proclaimed was not meant to convince by philosophical argument, but to demonstrate the convincing power

*of the Spirit, so that your faith should depend not on
human wisdom but on the power of God ... Now,
the Spirit we have received is not the spirit of the
world, but God's own Spirit, so that we may understand the lavish gifts God has given us. And these are
what we speak of, not in the terms learnt from human
philosophy, but in terms learnt from the Spirit, fitting
spiritual language to spiritual things.*

(1 Corinthians 2:1–5, 12–13)

I once had to go to a foot therapy class. We were
told to open and close our toes and to waggle them
independently of each other. My toes are like soldiers,
whatever the big toe does the rest follow in military
obedience. I complained to the therapist that it was
impossible for me to do what she was asking. She
simply replied: 'You have got the muscles, therefore
you can learn to use them.'

As we saw in the chapter on 'Praying through the
Spirit' every person has a spirit, but since we are not
able to see it, feel it, sense it, we tend to neglect it and
we pay much more attention to our bodies and minds.
If we neglect to use our spirit, then it, like muscles,
becomes all but paralysed. The Holy Spirit contacts us
through our spirit, but if we are out of touch with our
spirit, then we successfully block the Holy Spirit.

We can learn about God through our minds. We can
be taught truths about God. We can learn that he
created the world, he sent his Son to save us, he did
this through the cross and resurrection. But these
truths can just remain facts learnt but not life giving.
It is the Spirit of God that has to take these truths
and through his revelation to our spirit bring life to
something that could just remain an intellectual truth.

Ronald, in the story, experienced the Holy Spirit
illuminating truths that he already knew – but until

then it had just been a bit of knowledge, not something life giving. It was a gift of God to Ronald when he burst in to his life during that retreat. What was important, was that Ronald took this gift and began to work at it, developing it and letting it grow.

God deals with each of us as individuals and he knows how best to approach us. He drops us lots of little hints, which alas, we are often very lazy about. Sometimes he has, as it were, to shout to catch our attention. We can even abuse this and just enjoy the sudden flood of insights, but fundamentally remain unchanged. Ronald responded and so Ronald grew.

When Ronald found prayer becoming difficult, this was God again beginning to act. Everyone of us is born self-centred and even after God has awakened us and made us aware of him, we can still follow him for very selfish reasons. All that has happened is that our objective has changed – once it was material things, now it is spiritual – but self is still in the driving seat. God, in his own time, knows when to start correcting us. This cannot be rushed, we cannot cause it to happen – try being forgetful of self and you will soon see the problem.

The way God has to do it is to make us aware of our poverty, our shallowness, our sinfulness. When prayer becomes difficult, God is asking us 'Are you here for me or for you?' If we give up prayer because we no longer 'get anything out of it' then clearly we were praying for self-centred reasons. The whole prayer experience is a journey into God away from self. Our very way of being is to be centred on ourself. We see everything from where we are; we cannot even begin to imagine what it looks like from where God is, until God begins to show us. This is a moment of crisis and many who meet it give up praying and become busy affirming themselves, doing something they can claim credit for.

God made us for himself. Therefore the self is good. But we stole the self from God and made it into ego. We said 'I want me for me' and we live in the illusion that one day we will find total satisfaction in the 'me'. There is no escape from this prison, until we allow the one who became a man and never lived for the 'me' to set us free. 'Unless a wheat grain falls into the earth and dies, it remains only a single grain' (John 12:24). There has to come a dying and it is not a dying that we arrange. We can practise great self-effacement, we can learn to sit in the lowest seat, but the ego can flourish on such a diet. It is only when Jesus calls us into the fire of the cross, can he cause death and resurrection.

Let's face it, a prayer life can be sought after because we think that will put us among the special ones. We must remember that 'Blessed are the poor in spirit' — we are blessed when we fail, when we cannot pray, when we see the sin within ourselves, when we have nothing to boast of save that he who fashioned rainbows also made us and can and will refashion us in his time. Maybe he is delaying that refashioning until we, having died, will not take any of his glory for ourselves.

FOR REFLECTION

1. Do you judge your prayer by how much you get out of it?
2. What do you do when prayer becomes dry? Examine your conscience? Slog on? Review your ways of praying?
3. Are you content simply to be in his presence? This does not mean necessarily that you will feel it, but are you content just to know he is there?

PRAYER

Lord, no thought or idea I have ever had of you, is you.
You are greater than any thought of mine could ever
dream up. I want, not thoughts of you, I want you.
Come! Yet, as I say that I know you have come. Amen.

Praying through the Church

■━━■

AN AMERICAN WOMAN is reported to have said: 'Sure, I love God, but I'm not nuts about him.' Most of us, I am sure, know only too well what she means, but we would not have put it quite in that way.

We live in a world where every form of experience is now available and I wonder if our senses have become over stimulated, over-fed, so that they can no longer be satisfied with the normal and people are ever on the look out for something new, something more powerful. 'I'm bored, what's new' is a cry often heard. Clearly to keep up with this demand is going to prove ever more impossible, for we cannot go on finding new sensations and experiences.

My prayer life started, as most people's, with seeing prayer as asking God for my wants and needs. Even when I prayed the rosary, I was saying these prayers for an intention and I was not doing as I should, pondering all that Christ had done for my salvation. I was just saying some Our Fathers many Hail Marys and a few Glory bes, in the hope that many prayers would get a better hearing.

School retreats, with their imposed silences, did leave me with questions as to how to occupy the silence. Clearly one could not fill them with endless petitions. I think most of us solved this problem by reading lives of saints. I remember one book I read was about a young French boy who had visions of Our Lady. This set me longing for a vision and I remember going into the church one night after supper when all was dark. I settled myself in the Lady Chapel to await my vision. I do not remember what I said while I waited. In the church there was an old organ and before anyone played it its power had to be turned on. This would sound like the rushing of a great wind. Unknown to me someone came into the church to practise the organ, and when I heard the mighty wind, I was out of that church before you could have said 'Holy Smoke', and away down the school passage like a scalded cat. So much for my vision.

I am amazed now at my ignorance of the basic Christian truths. I do not blame anyone for this ignorance, because I have been a teacher and I know how people can just not hear you. My idea of God was more of a disciplinarian than a loving father. I can see quite easily how a person could pick up such an idea. The trouble is that once an idea has come to rest, all other ideas can be coloured by it.

Prayers in church went over my head. I was not praying prayers of thanksgiving, I was not adoring God for the gift of his Son, I was not asking that his death and resurrection should affect my life. I was asking for favours, so nothing I heard in church touched my world.

In those days the Mass was in Latin and that did not help. It is true I had a missal, and I learnt to follow in English, but even the English was not my everyday language – it all seemed so foreign. So no wonder I was bored and alas, I expected to be bored, because God did not seem to appear in my life or even be a bit interested in it.

◀▬▬▶

'Be careful not to forget Yahweh your God, by neglecting his commandments, customs and laws which I
am laying down for you today. When you have eaten
all you want, when you have built fine houses to live
in, when you have seen your flocks and herds increase,
your silver and gold abound and all your possessions
grow great, do not become proud of heart. Do not
then forget Yahweh your God who brought you out of
Egypt, out of the place of slave-labour, who guided
you through this vast and dreadful desert, a land of
fiery snakes, scorpions, thirst; who in this waterless
place brought you water out of the flinty rock; who
in this desert fed you with manna unknown to your
ancestors, to humble you and test you and so make
your future the happier.

'Beware of thinking to yourself, "My own strength
and the might of my own hand have given me the
power to act like this." Remember Yahweh your God;
he was the one who gave you the strength to act
effectively like this, thus keeping then, as today, the
covenant which he swore to your ancestors. Be sure:
if you forget Yahweh your God, if you follow other
gods, if you serve them and bow down to them – I
testify to you today – you will perish. Like the nations
Yahweh is to destroy before you, so you yourselves
will perish, for not having listened to the voice of
Yahweh your God.'

(Deuteronomy 8:11–20)

◀▬▬▶

Church is not theatre, and just as the Jews had an
obligation to teach their sons the meaning behind the
family ceremonies celebrated each Sabbath, so Christians need to educate their children in what Church
ceremonies stand for. If we have not been grounded in

the fact that Jesus stood in for us when he died then
we will wonder why the Church constantly talks about
the death of Christ. We may find it morbid, rather
depressing, could even get guilty feelings about it; but
once we have seen the love that drove Jesus to accept
suffering in our place, we will find that it becomes an
event we do not want to forget. But Jesus did more
than die in our place, he rose up from the dead and
has become the new Adam and he wants us to allow
him to live in us thus enabling us to live in a new
way.

The Church is God's instrument whereby he continues to care for us. It is made up of fallible people,
through whom the Holy Spirit brings to perfection
all that Jesus achieved for us through his death and
resurrection. In the course of the year the Church calls
to mind the great events whereby Christ won eternal
life for us. Before Christmas we wait as the chosen
people waited all those centuries for the promised
Messiah. This sense of expectancy reminds us that
Jesus is coming again. We are urged to long for his
return, not so that our troubles will be over, but so
that the great work of Jesus will be completed. He will
receive due honour and glory. Many of us have quite
a long way to grow before we can honestly say we look
forward to heaven, not as a place where we will be
totally happy, but as a place where God's plans will
have been totally fulfilled.

At Christmas, we ponder the mystery how God
became man. We will never be able to fathom this
mystery. How can he who is everywhere be suddenly
confined to somewhere? How can he who is all powerful be suddenly limited? How can he who knows everything ever learn?

During Lent, Easter and Pentecost we continue to
ponder the mystery of Christ dying and rising from the
dead. We try and grasp the evil of sin, we celebrate our

reconciliation with the Father and praise God for the sending of his Holy Spirit.

In doing this the Church is teaching us how to pray. Prayer is more than petition, it is the praising of God for his mighty being, his marvellous creation and his saving power. Every time we call to mind what God has done for us, we are affected more and more deeply by that saving event. To help us pray the Church puts Scripture before us where we hear what God has done, and then puts psalms on our lips so that we respond to these great acts of God. Praying with the Church is not just saying prayers, it is praying with meaning the prayers that are spoken during services. Signs and symbols are used to illustrate meanings more deeply. Music and songs are used to help us worship God.

FOR REFLECTION

1. In our personal prayer time, do we do as the Church does when it prays?
2. Do you find the prayers the Church puts on our lips often express very well the sentiments that are in our hearts?
3. Is your spiritual life very personal and private? Do you object to others being with you at Mass?

PRAYER

Jesus, I thank you for your church. I thank you for the wisdom you have given her ever since you founded her. I bless you for the way you have shaped her through pain, questionings, open rebellion and persecution. Help me to learn through her wisdom. Teach me to listen to all that she has learnt. I thank you for the many whose lives have enriched her understanding. Give me a love for your Church. Never let me be a cause for her blushing. Amen.

Praying through the Word

◆━━━◆

IT IS QUITE EASY to see now how I grew up fearing God. I learned that he was good, that he wanted me to be good; I was told that he was almighty and therefore could do anything he wished. I also learnt that he could be angry, that he caused the flood, sent fiery serpents among his people when they made a golden calf to be worshipped. In my mind's eye I can still see some of the horrific pictures in the book we had of Old Testament stories depicting these terrible events. So, all in all, I learnt many conflicting truths about God, and that made him very confusing and mysterious.

I suppose what affected me most was the way I experienced God. Since he was good and almighty I asked him for favours. I would ask for a variety of things. For picnics and days out I would ask for fine weather. Exams always seemed to be looming and that would get me to lengthen my prayers. In our family I heard of troubles and problems afflicting relatives, so prayers for their intentions were said. Life has many difficulties and so all these intentions, plus deliverance from school terms, were put before this all powerful God. Not many of my prayers seemed to get answered, so in my boyish heart, I came to the conclusion that if this God is almighty and he does not use his mighty

power to help me, then I cannot figure very high in
his estimation.

I now see a sharp distinction between what I learnt
about God and how I experienced him. No matter how
another person is described to you, if you experience
them differently, then that counts far more than what
anyone says. I feel this is significant for it explains to
me how I could not take in the positive teachings that
I must have heard.

Our minds become set and it takes a long time and
much effort before they can be shifted. I do not think
I would have admitted to having a fear of God for it is
quite possible to have an attitude and be quite blind
to it. My life was not evil, I went to church, I practised
the gospel reasonably well, I said my prayers and was
a respectable citizen. So I did not see how things really
were in my life, and that I had a fear of God.

Today, even after understanding something of this
problem, I can still react in situations of tension with
feelings of resentment against God. For instance, I hate
rushing to be on time. I like to leave myself plenty of
leeway. Thus if trains are late, or traffic is heavy, I
become tense. I find myself saying: 'Come on Lord,
get the train to come.' Or, 'Lord, keep that light green
until I get there.' And I get all uptight if he does not
answer with what I want. Deep down I still want to
blame him, and that is very foolish and it is a very
wrong attitude towards this loving God. Later I will
explain how I try to deal with this.

The point I am trying to make is how early
impressions of God can penetrate very deep, and if
these impressions are wrong, they can do an immense
amount of damage. Having had to counsel a number
of people, I can say these basic attitudes are quite
common and they can successfully block us from the
truth about God. God has given us a remedy, he has
spoken the truth to us and we must seriously ask

ourselves if we allow our lives to be shaped by these revelations.

Do not be afraid, for I have redeemed you;
I have called you by your name, you are mine.

(Isaiah 43:1)

I shall pour clean water over you and you will be cleansed . . . I shall give you a new heart, and put a new spirit in you.

(Ezekiel 36:25–26)

'It is not the healthy who need the doctor, but the sick. I came to call not the upright, but sinners.'

(Mark 2:17)

'Come to me, all you who labour and are over-burdened, and I will give you rest. Shoulder my yoke and learn from me, for I am gentle and humble in heart, and you will find rest for your souls. Yes, my yoke is easy and my burden light.'

(Matthew 11:28–30)

I found a way out of the problem of wrong images of God through someone who began to explain the story of the Fall for me. As a child, I had accepted the story as it was; it was only much later that I began to question it. I felt a bit hard done by that I, and the rest of humanity, should have to suffer for Adam and Eve's wrong action. It did not seem fair. Later on I grew quite sceptical about the early chapters of Genesis and felt it was a rather naive way to explain the problem of suffering and evil in the world. Because these early chapters seemed irrelevant I did not pay much attention to them.

I can now see that Satan was repeating in me the same strategy that he had used against Adam and Eve. As these chapters were opened to me, I began to see that they were not irrelevant. This was the way Satan still acted today.

Satan set out to undermine Adam and Eve's confidence in God. His plan was to undermine their trust. He starts by asking an innocent question: 'Did God really say you were not to eat from any of the trees in the garden?' Eve replies that it was only from the tree in the middle of the garden that they were forbidden to eat. Here Satan craftily sows doubt. He suggests that God's command, not to eat from the tree of knowledge of good and evil, was because God feared that Adam and Eve would become like him and rival him. Doubt was put into Eve's heart – 'perhaps this God was not so good after all? Perhaps he did not want their growth and development?' It is tragic to think that she was moved to listen to this unknown serpent and take his word rather than the word of the one they knew and with whom they walked.

Satan is in the business of making God look unfavourable and untrustworthy. Ask people what they think about God, and most will have some pretty nasty suspicions about him.

Once I began to see and recognise the wound that the Fall had left in me, I began to see how to deal with Satan. He wanted me to mistrust God, so when God did not grant my every wish, Satan played on that fact, lying to me by saying that God did not love me. The trouble was, I had no firm trust in God; I relied more on what I felt or what I thought.

Today, because I have learnt bad habits, I have to take a firm control of the way I think in times of frustration. It is amazing how when I am in a hurry, things go wrong as though they are out to mess things up. I either lose the keys of the car, or mislay my glasses. The traffic lights change just as I reach them or I get behind a farm tractor and cannot get a chance to over-take. I have to stop myself reacting in my usual way of thinking of God sitting up in heaven waiting to do miracles on demand, but refusing to because he wants to try me out.

Slowly I have come to realise that my pictures of God had come from my feelings or my thoughts. I felt disappointed he did not answer my prayers, so I concluded he was not too interested in me. What I needed was a thorough grounding in what God had said about himself. I have had to take texts from Scripture, texts that tell of the goodness of God and I have had to ponder them, tell him I believe them, and then during the day I have tried to believe them. It has not been easy. Some days are better than others, others are disasters. But, slowly and gradually, I have found some progress has been made.

This is why I see prayer as a dialogue. I like to look at what God has said and then work at trying to believe it. It is not a question of working up one's feelings, or brainstorming, I just repeat the truth and tell God I want to believe it. I thank him for it, and try to live it. I have to admit many failures, but I know I have grown over the years. One day the full effect of his work on Calvary will come to fruition in me. I know I am not able to set myself free, but I also know I have to work along with him who strengthens me.

FOR REFLECTION

1. Is prayer a dialogue for you? If so, who does the speaking first?
2. Do you read the word of God apart from what you hear in church?
3. Would you say there is a difference between Bible study and praying the Scriptures?

4. What do you do when you seem not able to pray?
5. If you find it hard to trust God, try repeating to yourself the Scripture passages printed in this chapter. If necessary, make this a regular thing.

PRAYER

I praise you God that you are not a God of silence. I may not hear your voice, but I have your word and every time I read that I hear you speak. I bless you for all the ways you communicate with me. Lord, keep me wide awake, so that when you come to collect me, I shall be waiting. Amen.